Understanding Emotional Intelligence
in a week

JILL DANN

Hodder & Stoughton

A MEMBER OF THE HODDER HEADLINE GROUP

the Institute of Management

The Institute of Management (IM) is the leading
organisation for professional management. Its purpose is
to promote the art and science of management in every
sector and at every level, through research, education,
training and development, and representation of
members' views on management issues.
This series is commissioned by IM Enterprises Limited,
a subsidiary of the Institute of Management, providing
commercial services.

**Management House,
Cottingham Road,
Corby,
Northants NN17 1TT
Tel: 01536 204222;
Fax: 01536 201651
Website: http://www.inst-mgt.org.uk**

Registered in England no 3834492
Registered office: 2 Savoy Court, Strand,
London WC2R 0EZ

Orders: please contact Bookpoint Ltd, 130 Milton Park, Abingdon, Oxon
OX14 4SB.
Telephone: (44) 01235 400414, Fax: (44) 01235 400454. Lines are open from
9.00–6.00, Monday to Saturday, with a 24 hour message answering service.
Email address: orders@bookpoint.co.uk

British Library Cataloguing in Publication Data
A catalogue record for this title is available from The British Library

ISBN 0 340 80210 3

First published	2001
Impression number	10 9 8 7 6 5 4 3 2 1
Year	2005 2004 2003 2002 2001

Cover photograph from Telegraph Colour Library.

Typeset by SX Composing DTP, Rayleigh, Essex.
Printed in Great Britain for Hodder & Stoughton Educational, a division of
Hodder Headline Plc, 338 Euston Road, London NW1 3BH. by
Cox & Wyman Ltd, Reading, Berkshire.

■■■■ C O N T E N T S ■■■■

Experts are beginning to agree that types of intelligence other than IQ (Intelligence Quotient) have evolved in humans over the last two million years. A high IQ is not enough to guarantee success in life. When you have a high EQ (Emotional Intelligence Quotient) you are adept at interpreting the emotional roots of your own thinking and behaviour and *choosing* your actions to influence outcomes. You are also capable of making good insights into the behaviour and reactions of others.

For many leading companies in the UK, Emotional Intelligence (EI) has become the core of soft skills competencies and management development. The emerging Emotional Intelligence movement in this country seeks to encourage modern humans to utilise the advantages of brain design that they had as cave-people in order to brave the challenges of the 21st century.

Whereas IQ is more or less a given, EQ can be increased by a significant commitment to your own development. The distinction is about your way of *being* not of *doing*. Improvement cannot be achieved solely by attending a training course or reading a book to acquire knowledge.

There is no single view of what EI is; there are a number of different views (as with many management topics). Daniel Goleman, one well-known author, defines EI as:

> The capacity for recognising our own feelings and those of others, for motivating ourselves, and for managing emotions well in ourselves and in our relationships.

INTRODUCTION

Most people spend more time than they would like obsessing about situations where they handled someone badly (eg lost control or misunderstood others). Businesses lose money because of time wasted in this process. Equally, efficiency and effectiveness can be improved by mastering relationship skills with customers, suppliers and staff.

Leadership requires excellent self-awareness, self-control, awareness of others and social skills. Purposefully developing these EI competencies can have a startling effect on personal and business success.

There are several models and definitions of EI, which have their own measurement and assessment tools. If this seems confusing, don't panic; you would not be happy if you only had one choice of holiday, new lawnmower or type of food. We will explore them each day as they become most useful to the topic under discussion. So, shop around by looking at all these models to:

1. Decide whether you even want to bother trying to develop your EQ at all beyond its present level, as part of other complementary priorities such as development of professional skills and knowledge.

2. Decide whether there is a match in one of these approaches to your own particular values, beliefs and attitudes or very tangible things such as the company competency framework.

3. Start to build a picture of situations in your life that can be alleviated by managing them in a more emotionally intelligent way. This will help you to complete your Personal Development Plan (PDP) in the final chapter.

This book looks at the main areas that EI touches in everyday life and in business life.

The week ahead comprises:

Sunday	What is EI and EQ?
Monday	Becoming more self-aware
Tuesday	Generating an Internal Observer
Wednesday	Stress management and EI
Thursday	What will my company gain from an investment in EI?
Friday	How to create an EI culture
Saturday	Preparing for the next developmental steps

What is EI and EQ?

Today, we are going to gain an understanding of:

- What is Emotional Intelligence?
- EI is learnable
- When you get emotionally hijacked
- Measurement of EQ
- How EI will change you
- Where we see EI in everyday situations
- Keeping a journal

What is Emotional Intelligence?

EI is complementary to intellectual intelligence, the purely cognitive, innate capacities measured by your IQ. IQ is not undermined by EQ. Also, since much of brain function is still being discovered, EI may be just another one of many forms of intelligence that we are discovering or beginning to understand.

Modern thinking is that there are views of intelligence that distinguish particularly gifted individuals in mathematics, music, artistic ability, management and technology. EI describes abilities distinct from these more academic or intellectual intelligences. Intellectual and Emotional Intelligence derive from different parts of the brain so they function in different ways.

Intellect (cognition or thinking) is based on the workings of the Cerebral Cortex (3rd Brain), the more recently evolved layers at the top of the brain. Emotions are controlled by the more ancient Subcortex (2nd Brain), a lower part of the brain.

Modern neuroscience tells us that the emotional centre of the brain learns differently than the cognitive centre. We can learn to fine-tune, or increase our use of, different parts of the human brain.

By understanding what it is and equally what it is not, you can apply some of the understanding to alleviate problems and generate new ideas. By applying the suggestions you will have started developing your own Emotional Intelligence. Raising your EQ to reduce and eliminate unproductive behaviour is rarely completed in one step. Some suggested steps are described throughout the week. You can decide to go further by completing the Personal Development Plan in Saturday's chapter.

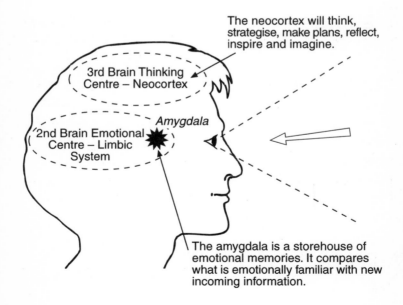

The neocortex will think, strategise, make plans, reflect, inspire and imagine.

3rd Brain Thinking Centre – Neocortex

Amygdala

2nd Brain Emotional Centre – Limbic System

The amygdala is a storehouse of emotional memories. It compares what is emotionally familiar with new incoming information.

EI is learnable

Raising EQ is possible because EI is learnable. First, what ways of learning do you find most helpful? Only you will know if you need to find out more about how you learn best. If you have not thought about how you learn best, what the options are and how to explore your preferences, then I suggest you set up a period of enquiry. We will cover this on Saturday as an option at the start of your EI Personal Development Plan.

Learning ladder rung number	What it feels like when you are on it
1 Unconscious incompetence	You do not know what you do not know
2 Conscious incompetence	You now know what you do not know and you may not like it
3 Conscious competence	You know what you know and feel clumsy practising this new-found knowledge or skill
4 Unconscious competence	You feel as if you have always known this or been proficient in this skill

If you are really in tune with your needs you will find it easier to tackle the kind of learning involved in raising your EQ.

Two types of learning
We have postulated that there are two basic types of learning:

- **Cognitive.** Cognitive learning is about absorbing new data and insights into existing frameworks of association and understanding. We also need to engage that part of the brain where our emotional signature is stored. Changing habits, such as learning to approach people positively rather than avoiding them, learning to listen better or to give feedback skillfully, is much more challenging than simply adding new data to old.
- **Emotional.** Emotional learning involves that and more. Emotional learning involves new ways of thinking and acting that are more in tune with our identity – our values; and beliefs and attitudes. If you are told to learn a new word-processing program, you will probably get on with it; however, if you are told that you need to improve control of your temper, you are likely to be upset or offended. So the prospect of needing to develop greater emotional intelligence is likely to generate resistance to change.

Remember what it was like when you first learned to drive a car? You did not know what you did not know. Do you remember what effect the way your instructor treated you had on your ability to retain the lessons and on your self-confidence? Alternatively, do you remember just after buying a new car, having to retrain yourself in how to switch on the lights without having to think consciously where they were located. Getting to do these things at the 'unconscious competence' level involves building a new neural pathway in your brain.

As we go through the week I will set you voluntary exercises each day, designed to deepen your understanding of what it feels like to develop your EI.

When you get emotionally hijacked

Consider this. You've had a long and exhausting day visiting some stunning parts of the country on holiday touring India. You arrive back to the campsite, enjoy an excellent meal but leave fellow travellers to party around the roaring campfire. You retire early and fall into a deep sleep. Suddenly wide-awake, you sit bolt upright to be confronted with a tiger looming over you.

It's so close that all you can see are its eyes. You have an immediate and very strong emotional reaction, which causes you to do one of three things (and maybe some others too!):

1   you freeze; or

2   you leap out of bed and run like mad; or

3   you throw something at the offending animal.

You have just experienced an amygdala hijack: Freeze, Flight or Fight. Early humans relied on the automatic 'Freeze, Flight or Fight' reactions for their survival when confronted with danger. If Darwin is correct, we are the progeny of those ancestors who successfully utilised the Freeze, Flight or Fight reaction. They survived better than the rest.

> The ancient brain centers for emotion also harbor the skills needed for managing ourselves effectively and for social adeptness. Thus these skills are grounded in our evolutionary heritage for survival and adaptation.
> Daniel Goleman's, *Working with Emotional Intelligence* (1998).

Let's look at what happened. Your reaction is an instantaneous adrenaline-based reaction and has no cognitive thought associated with it. It is an emotional hijack because the Subcortex or reptilian brain (2nd Brain) processes reactions some 80,000 times faster than the Cerebral Cortex (3rd Brain) processes thoughts.

How can we take advantage of this faster processing? The greater speed is beneficial when we use it to make better decisions using wide-ranging soft (emotional, intuitive) information as well as the traditional hard (cognitive, knowledge-based) data. It is powerful when we pick up information from all our senses and use it to manage relationships and social situations more perceptively.

Implications in a business environment
To survive, we developed a reaction that was appropriate to the situations that Early Man encountered, where we were physically threatened. Now, let's consider the inappropriateness of using this response in modern business. Seeing the tiger, you moved from low to very high arousal designed to give you some choices in survival. Now, let's take away the tiger and immerse ourselves in everyday

normal situations. You are likely to have had several close-call situations causing an adrenaline rush. When the boss says, 'I want to see you in my office in five minutes', do we carefully consider all the possible reasons why? No, we immediately assume we are in trouble and panic.

Your body is primed for action and is reacting with the fight reactions of anger, aggression and hostility or the flight/freeze emotions of fear, anxiety and nervousness. It is stressful not to be able to release the energy provided through the fight or flight physical activity expected. This lack of release causes many illnesses.

Today, there are generally fewer threats to our personal safety. The main threats that we perceive are of a financial, emotional, mental and social nature. These types of threats are constantly present in our environment and are not generally dealt with immediately.

Measurement of EQ

Much emphasis is placed on measurement of EQ (obviously by the vendors of the half dozen or so instruments). This gives individuals information about their own competence either through self-scoring or, more recently, through 360° instruments (reverse appraisal of managers, feedback from peers as well as seniors). My recommendation is that the reader should focus on development and not become hooked on measurement alone. By focusing on development of EI, individuals, teams and organisations can reap transformational change. By designing training in specific ways, it is possible to do without an assessment and to role-play good EI and bad EI situations. However, I recommend having some form of assessment at the beginning and one year into the developmental process, with the emphasis on using the information for improvements, not just for providing a snapshot of where you are.

Development of any kind is slow or difficult when an individual has low self-awareness. EI training and development is an approach that (usually) starts with raising the self-awareness of the individual. Self-awareness is something that is notoriously difficult to train. It has to be part of a developmental process over a managed period of time usually following a pattern of input, reflection and discovery.

How EI will change you

Personal impact of low EQ
You may well feel better mentally and physically – I know I do. It would also be perfectly normal to have lapses back to some unhelpful behaviour. However, you would have better information about why that happened and be able to take steps to prevent a recurrence.

- We are worried, anxious and confused about priorities.
- We are time-pressured, inefficient and perform poorly.
- We are tired, fatigued and frustrated.
- We have a poor work–life balance.
- We may have elevated blood pressure.
- We age more quickly.

If you invest in a significant developmental process you will prepare for, conduct and reflect on day-to-day challenges in new ways – possibly with startling results. People might say to you that you look less stressed or that you do not overreact to previous 'hot buttons'. You may feel more grown-up and happier.

I have direct experience of a year-long development programme in my own company which has:

- changed me and how I am with myself for the better
- enabled me to bear much greater stress and take more risks than I could before, with much reduced anxiety
- changed for the better how we function as a team
- increased the advocacy, referrals and quality of testimonials that we receive from clients
- improved how we communicate with suppliers and deal with complaints
- helped us to set achievable goals that align our personal lives with business ambitions.

Where we see EI in everyday situations

We will go through a number of everyday examples and exercises throughout the week.

The main areas that EI touches are:

- self-awareness, self-control, social skills and awareness of others
- business relationships with customers or clients, staff, managers, shareholders, suppliers, the local community and competitors
- sales and marketing technologies, which need emotionally intelligent approaches
- the trust radius that people have between each other at work.

- the effectiveness of teams working together under pressure
- the amount of initiative and the number of good ideas employees share with their company, leading to increased profit and reflected rewards
- increasing positive affirmation which can create physical and mental well-being
- giving and receiving negative feedback
- Continuous Professional Development (CPD) – it takes serious commitment to take time out for your own development. It is easy to let three months go by in a blink and to do nothing for your CPD. Taking a more emotionally intelligent approach to yourself and to how you prioritise your 'me time' can aid this.

The cost of low EQ

Think for a moment of three examples of situations where you have had a strong emotional response to others' behaviour:

- in a face-to-face encounter as a customer with a supplier, such as in a shop or at a supermarket checkout
- by email
- through a telephone conversation or Computer Telephony Integration system.

Write down the emotions you experienced and if there were any flashbacks to previous experiences.

- How did you respond to or behave towards them?
- How did you feel afterwards?
- Was there any further action or reaction (eg a letter of praise or complaint)?

Keeping a journal

I recommend that you start a journal which we will use throughout the week and conclude with on Saturday. The idea is consistently to log your learning, to make this as easy as possible and to keep the information in one place, readily to hand. I still find a bound notebook the best, despite my use of hand-held and other computer technology.

Keeping the journal will allow you to prepare for meetings and note your feelings and thoughts or expectations of the event. Making a record while the memory is fresh will give you the benefit of better quality reflection. Your preferred learning style may be more energetic activity than reflection. However, rounding off learning styles is good development in itself. If you stick to your natural one or two styles of learning you may miss out on more information. Try and stick to keeping the journal; it only takes a few weeks to form a good habit.

I keep a single book that includes my work notes as well and I do not worry about losing it (but I do not advertise the content). At least once a year, I review the content quickly writing up my conclusions on my reflections, plus any follow-up activity, in my latest journal. Very often I find little gems of advice that I have been given, which I have missed or not yet actioned.

Journal format

If you use the following format with some academic rigour, you might be able to include the material as part of a suitable qualification (such as management learning or organisational development). General rules are to:

- date the entry
- give some context (why, where and with whom); give anything relevant about the timing, such as an annual appraisal interview or someone's retirement party
- give details of the environment that affected the quality of the experience
- note anything that interferes with your ability to focus on the business at hand (you may be participating in a meeting, listening to a presentation or giving a coaching session etc)
- note anything that interferes with your relationship(s) with other participants
- note anything that interferes with the role you play (chairperson, coach etc).

Each day, I am going to give you exercises throughout the day and at the end. They are voluntary, but I recommend that you experience EI development before making any judgements about its use.

Becoming more self-aware

Today, we are going to gain an understanding of the following topics:

- Another Intelligence
- Raising self-awareness
- Self-awareness competencies
- The importance of emotions
- Journal entries:
- What relevence does EI have to me?
- What benefits will I accrue personally?

Another Intelligence

Dr John (Jack) D Mayer and Peter Salovey are thought to be the originators of the theory that there are intelligences other than IQ, published in a series of scientific literature in 1990. In particular, they develop the idea of Emotional Intelligence. Dr Mayer views EI as:

> A psychological capacity for making sense of and using emotional information. As individuals we will all have different innate capacities for doing this and we can learn from life how to improve it through effort, practice and experience.

They believe that EI really is an intelligence which can be reliably and objectively measured and that emotions can help our cognition and that thinking can help our emotions. They distinguish themselves from other thinkers who focus on social *skills*, or on outcomes, such as improved teambuilding, or on personality traits, such as optimism and outlook.

'Heart and head combined

> It is very important to understand that EI is not the opposite of intelligence, it is not the triumph of head over heart – it is the unique intersection of both. Emotional Intelligence combines emotion with intelligence . . .

> . . . In this view, emotion and thinking work together: emotion assists thinking, and thinking can be used to analyse emotion. EI then is the ability to use your emotions to help solve problems and live a more effective life . . .

> . . . Emotions are nagging thoughts. Emotions are very often unwelcome guests in our lives. Yet, emotions provide us with information, which if ignored, can cause serious problems. If we are aware of our emotions, if we act on our emotions in a rational way, then we will increase the odds in our favour.'

Mayer & Salovey, Chicago EI Conference paper,
September 1999

Raising self-awareness

The impact of increasing self-awareness

Self-awareness means that we are aware of what we think and feel in the present. This really is the core of EI. If you developed your EI, starting with increased self-awareness, what effect would it have:

- at home?
- in life?
- at work?

If you like, take a few moments to think of examples where you show heightened self-awareness and where you showed more limited awareness. I recommend that you write this down in your journal. We will use this on Saturday.

Common examples of heightened self-awareness would be:

- becoming aware of your present driving style and the impact it is having on other motorists
- being aware that you feel uncomfortable around a person, although not necessarily being aware why
- being aware of a pattern of unhelpful behaviour; knowing when you are repeating it and being aware you are starting down a well-worn path and are unable to stop it.

Write down at least two instances where you exhibited the same pattern of unhelpful behaviour and we will use this tomorrow.

Your learning curve from self-awareness to social adeptness
- To be self-aware you need to be emotionally literate – able to distinguish and label accurately individual emotions (see Tuesday).

- The next step is to become increasingly capable of self-control regardless of the emotions triggered by a situation.
- You then learn to increase your choices of behaviour in given situations.
- You can go on developmentally to use this to become more aware of others, their triggers and the emotional roots of their unhelpful behaviours.
- Finally, as you choose to develop, you become very socially adept using your self-awareness, self-regulation and awareness of others.
- You may elect to go on further acquiring knowledge about different cultures and customs. A goal may be to manage your reaction to unexpected clashes in moral, ethical and sociocultural standards. Another goal could be to use your increased EQ in coaching others, such as in culture change programmes (see Friday).

Self-awareness competencies

My personal view of what it takes to be self-aware is summarised in the following check box.

Self-awareness competencies

Emotional Awareness: Recognising one's emotions and their effects

People with this competence:
- ☐ know which emotions they are feeling, can name why and label them
- ☐ realise the chain from emotion to action (links between their feelings and what they think, do and say)

❏ recognise how their feelings affect their
   performance, the quality of experience at work and
   in relationships
❏ have a guiding awareness of their values or goals
   and any gap between espoused values and actual
   behaviour.

Accurate self-assessment: Knowing one's key strengths and limits

People with this competence are:
❏ aware of their strengths, weaknesses and emotional
   boundaries in relationships
❏ reflective, understanding the power of learning from
   experience even if reflection is not their natural style
❏ open to candid feedback, new perspectives,
   continuous learning and self-development
❏ objective about feedback from others and able to
   generate positive strokes for themselves
   appropriately
❏ able to show a sense of humour and perspective
   about themselves.

Self-confidence: Sureness about one's self-worth and capabilities

People with this competence:
❏ present themselves with self-assurance; have
   'presence' with warmth
❏ can celebrate diversity in teams, voice views that are
   unpopular and go out on a limb for what is right
❏ are decisive, able to make sound judgements using
   emotional and cognitive information despite
   uncertainties (perceptions of risk) and pressures.

Self-awareness competencies exercise

Note the answers to the following in your journal.
- Which of the above competencies do you feel represent your strengths?
- Why?
- How do you feel about those competencies?
- How would you practice and develop them:
- ❏ at home?
- ❏ in life?
- ❏ at work?

The importance of emotions

Before the benefits of high EQ can be grasped, the bedrock of EI is acknowledgement of the importance of emotions in business as well as personal life.

The importance of emotions

- our bodies communicate with us and others to tell us what we need
- the better our communication, the better we feel
- emotions help us establish our boundaries
- emotions have the potential to unite and connect us
- emotions can serve as our inner moral and ethical compass
- emotions are essential for good decision-making.

Look at the suggested importance of emotions and log what you think and feel in your journal. If you have problems distinguishing thoughts from emotions, delay doing the exercise until you have read Tuesday. You may like to share the reflection and debate with a friend or colleague.

Our bodies communicate with us through instinct, intuition and responses to Stressors in our lives. This information is of equal importance to our thought processes. How many times have you gone against a gut feeling to discover it has turned out to be true and you could not find a rational reason why?

We feel powerful when our communication is congruent and aligned inwardly. Conversely, when communication breaks down we are preoccupied and unable to concentrate on other things.

When you become self-aware and emotionally literate, you are able to distinguish single emotions triggered unexpectedly by some event. This can help you become aware of a personal boundary (what you can take and what you cannot endure). You then need to decide what to do with this insight to look after your emotional needs.

Emotions have the potential to unite and connect us – emotions can be catching. We are designed to achieve rapport with each other and to form bonds. We can achieve awesome targets when we are emotionally aligned with others.

Emotions can serve as our inner moral and ethical compass – tuning in precisely can help us with problem-solving. Sometimes employing purely analytical approaches using rational weightings does not serve us well. We need both rational and irrational information.

Emotions are essential for good decision-making – businesses are now beginning to accept that gut feeling and instinct has its place in making sound business decisions. Similarly in our private lives, when it comes to selecting a lifestyle option, the balance of advantages should include satisfying unmet emotional needs.

Journal entries

Do you recall someone who really moved you?

When you think about someone who really moved you, it is probably not so much that they *did* something different as that they had a way of *being* that was memorable. Writing in your learning journal, try doing this:
1 Think of someone warmly memorable in your life and just brainstorm keywords that paint a picture of how

they were with you, how they touched you and what it was like to be in their company.

2 Examine the list of characteristics you attributed to them. You will probably find that only one or two have anything to do with their IQ, if any. It is highly likely that the characteristics that influenced you are those falling into an Emotional Intelligence framework – self-awareness and self-regulation, awareness of others, social skills and good interpersonal communications.

The start of self-awareness is to test your readiness to change. Have you any motivation to change?

What relevance does EI have to me?
Tick all that apply. It will help you to know about EI if you are concerned with:

❑ your influencing skills; wanting to understand others more in terms of what persuades them, what they can actively listen to and really hear to be influenced
❑ stressful situations that get on top of you and that cause you to be anxious about them hours after they have occurred or which wake you up in the middle of the night
❑ getting the message across to people unambiguously and being able to listen without inner dialogue disrupting concentration
❑ your life–work balance because it must become more equitable and you need to renegotiate how your time is spent
❑ relationships that are stressful or even mystifying in terms of your behaviour or the reactions of others

❑ your general health being below what is accepted as a healthy norm and suspecting that it is self-inflicted injury in the form of bad habits, self-deprecation and lack of commitment.

Log in your journal any conclusions you reach about why EI is of interest or of use to you from the above list and your own ideas. Leave space to log more conclusions as they occur to you throughout the week.

What benefits will I accrue personally?

What benefits you will accrue personally will depend on your current level of EI and what challenges you are facing that need a higher EQ. However, throughout the week I give you examples of where I have personally benefited by my own company going through an EI development programme. I also include those reported by several clients. For example, a client asked us to come up with a way of raising self-awareness in a group of reasonably senior managers:

UK Financial plc EI Programme to raise self-awareness

- They read some pre-course material on the business case for EI and leadership.
- They completed an EI assessment and read guidance on how to interpret the results to plan development.
- They underwent a single but bespoke one-day EI development event, which integrated self-awareness competencies with their existing management development framework.
- They were supported during the three-month

---

development period back in the workplace by an HR
Partner and their line manager, each of whom had
been specifically prepared for their roles.
• They had a bespoke workbook for the course, which
had a separate section of post-course exercises
organised by relationship type and self-study. The
workbook also included information on enhancement
of learning.

The managers reported wide-ranging benefits for a
relatively small investment during an independent
evaluation three to four months after the initial event.
They claimed benefits ranging from 'transformational'
to a definite increase in specific self-awareness and
related competencies. The increases spanned a range
such as expressing themselves more effectively,
dealing with conflict and improving relationships at
work.

Plan your next step for raising your EI competencies using
this feedback. Tomorrow, we will look at building on
enhanced self-awareness by increasing our self-control
through the use of our inner voice.

Generating an internal observer

Today, we are going to gain an understanding of the following topics:

- Deconstructing and rebuilding reactions
- Taking control of your behavioural patterns
- Becoming emotionally literate
- Understanding the ABC model
- Moving from hindsight to foresight
- Competencies for self-control
- Journal entries

Deconstructing and rebuilding reactions

Humans experience a number of feelings at the same time or experience them as a chain of emotions. Tracking back through these provides powerful insights into unhelpful repeated behaviours. We need to become aware of a potential negative emotional reaction before it is happening. During or in the immediate aftermath of a negative emotional reaction, we need to take note of the triggers that caused it. By deconstructing these situations, we come to an understanding of why they happen. We learn the triggers so that when we next experience them, we intervene and choose another behaviour or just forget about it (ie we choose not to respond.)

You have to be able to intervene in your own thinking to be able to break bad habits. You need to pick up the emotions generated by given situations and work out where they came from. It is important to learn to distinguish emotions to get more information about what is driving you.

Do you have any patterns of repeated behaviour that do not make sense to you? Most people have some bad habits that they know do them no good.

We can train ourselves to react differently, to react positively and to use foresight rather than hindsight to manage our emotions. To be successful in this, we need to rehearse acquiring foresight frequently so that we become unconsciously competent in it. At this point, we react in a different manner without really thinking about it. Just like switching on the lights on our new car without fumbling.

Taking control of your behavioural patterns

Behavioural patterns are actions that you tend to do over and over in response to a particular situation. For example, when you get angry you shout, when impatient you may tap a pen on the table or swing your foot back and forth. Just as our thoughts are tied in with our emotions so our behaviour is also tied in.

So, to manage our emotions we need to take control of our behaviours and to do that we must first recognise them. Certain behaviours are generally associated with specific emotions, eg we approach people when we are enthusiastic, we sit around and do nothing when we are depressed and we fidget when anxious.

These of course are generalisations. If they go unchecked they perpetrate negative emotions. Often we don't notice our behaviour. A raised voice in response to anger or excitement means that we may not even be aware that we are doing it.

Becoming emotionally literate

We need to be able to identify our thoughts and our feelings separately, distinguishing and labelling emotions accurately. Several times so far in your life, you will have been asked to express your feelings. You may have found this difficult; most people express what they are thinking and not what they are feeling. This is not a trivial thing to do.

Recognising blanket emotions
Some feelings that we initially believe to be distinct are actually generated by a series of individual emotions. Given time to distinguish, these blanket emotions literally conceal a chain of single and distinct emotions, which provide us with enormous insights.

To develop your self-awareness you are going to develop a different part of your brain. It's like exercising a new muscle and it needs concentration. So to help you, here are a few simple rules that you can apply quickly and easily.

- To be sure that you are expressing feelings, start with the words, 'I feel . . .', and then add a feeling word. If you say, 'I feel *that* . . .' then you are actually expressing what you think. Use the following table of emotions to expand your vocabulary of emotion-related adjectives.
- Essentially, we have just four primary feelings: Mad, Sad, Glad and Scared (see table of suggestions). However, we use many different words to describe them.
- Feelings can also be complex. Some, known as blanket emotions, indicated by an asterisk (*) in the table, are composites of two or more primary feelings; eg, jealousy can comprise envy, fear, sadness, sense of loss etc. It is very important that you learn to distinguish the separate

emotions involved in complex emotions if you are to build the necessary new neural pathways to better outcomes.

• To express your thoughts, start with the words, 'I think . . .'.

MAD	SAD	GLAD	SCARED	OTHER
angry*	blue	amused	afraid	affectionate
annoyed*	depressed*	comfortable	agitated	bored*
ashamed	despondent	content	alone	closed
belittled*	discouraged	ecstatic	awkward	co-operative*
guilty	distressed	effervescent	concerned	dumb-founded*
irritated	down	elated	confused	loving
jealous*	down and out	excited	distressed	encouraged
disappointed	grief-sricken	fascinated	nervous	flummoxed*
discouraged	hurt	fulfilled	forgetful	forgiving
frustrated*	lonely	giddy	ignored*	fevered
furious*	left out	glorious	inhibited	guileful

Becoming able to label distinct emotions accurately allows us to examine the first time we experienced those emotions. Frequently, unhelpful behaviours in adults can be linked to interpretation during some past event. We experience a range of emotions during an incident and we make it mean something about ourselves, about our standards or place in the world. This interpretation is remembered and carried through inappropriately to later life.

We can use our increased self-awareness and ability at accurate self-assessment to revisit the first time these emotions were experienced. Visualising ourselves in the situation, we re-evaluate the significance to overcome any negative self-beliefs that were formed or beliefs about others. We can then choose a new response to the chain of emotions triggered by the situation should we encounter them again.

Before you can really get a grasp on why it is worth using EI as an approach for personal development and systemic culture changes in business, we need to go through some events in slow motion.

Emotional literacy

Using the previous table, write down a number of emotions that you are likely to experience in your workplace: anger, joy, anxiety, contentment, depression, enthusiasm, fear, confidence, sadness, frustration.
- What behavioural patterns accompany the emotions that you are most likely to encounter at work?
- For all of the emotions on your list, what are your corresponding behavioural actions?
- Explore any possible patterns. For example, you're afraid that you might be moved to another site but you also fear that your co-worker told your boss last week that you really didn't want to be part of this new set-up. You respond by doing everything you can to avoid running into your boss or co-worker.
- Look at your behavioural actions in response to other situations in your workplace.

Understanding and using the ABC Model (Affect, Behaviour & Cognition)

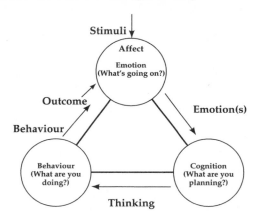

This model should be referred to as the ACB model as the flow is from emotion (Affect) to thought processes (Cognition) resulting in observed activity (Behaviour). Let me give you an example of a bad habit that I had before my EI coach helped me to distinguish where it came from.

Before EI development
I am away a lot in the course of my consultancy and training work. The office does not stand still while I am away – equipment and software will be upgraded or replaced. When I get back, I need to allow time to catch up and learn to use what is new. Inevitably, I experience time pressures to meet a deadline of some sort. However, I just want to use the office software and get on with completing things. Very often I have to ask for help because the software does not respond as it used to and I make mistakes.

My bad habit is being grumpy with the person who helps

me. It's not very nice doing this and I wasn't very proud of myself for doing so. Now there is no logic in doing this either. It is not rational to be difficult when someone is coming to your aid, nor was it something I planned to do.

During EI development
My EI coach suggested that I visualise being at the computer and at the point where I had to ask for help. He then persisted in asking me what my emotions were at the time.

I realised that I was angry but he did not let it rest there. Anger is a blanket emotion. It is not useful information in itself because you have nowhere to go with it. By persisting and making me stay in the moment, I understood that I felt jealous, humiliated, resentful and afraid.

The coach then asked about my past and if I could relate these emotions to anything. He framed it in such a way that I felt very adult about exploring it and not the least bit humiliated. It suddenly came to me that at a mainframe computer site where I had worked almost 20 years before, *I* used to be the person that people asked for expert help (on a particular computer language). I was not conscious of this having an impact on my self-esteem but clearly it had.

Let's look at the emotions concerning this.

- Jealousy – I am envious of the knowledge that whoever helps me has acquired.
- Humiliated – I am the expert not the apprentice. I feel stupid on software that I have previously been very adept at using.
- Resentful – I am out earning the money that paid for you (my helper) to gain this expertise.

- Afraid – I am scared that I am getting out of touch and that I will never catch up.
- Anger – I feel irritated and grumpy because of all the other feelings.

After EI development

Now, I appreciate that this is not a life-threatening situation and can appear trivial in the analysis. But the point is that I very quickly broke the bad habit and integrated the learning to look at other areas. On reflection, I was amazed at the range of emotions I had experienced. Rationally (external thinking) I had made being in need of induction training on changes in the office mean a whole range of things about me (internal feelings). It was only by deconstruction that I realised how futile this was. I felt invigorated by this discovery not humiliated.

The next time I started to get angry at the computer, I had a new 'warning light' appear in my head and I immediately felt very different about things – amused instead of angry. At first, I would be in the middle of starting down the well-worn neural pathway leading to me being grumpy with my helper. I became able to use my internal observer to break the chain.

Sharing the chain of emotions with my colleagues explained this mysterious behaviour to them. Since then I can have healthy adult-to-adult conversations about many behaviours that would have been difficult for me before. It also demonstrated to colleagues how the EI coaching process led me to some insights that they could use for their own behavioural issues.

Moving from hindsight to foresight

From the EI coaching I learned to acquire foresight about potential emotional reactions, by going through a learning curve with time. I learned:

- *Hindsight*, initially. Reflecting on the oucome, by considering the Affect and the emotions caused, I was able to rerun the events in my mind and decide to take any corrective action that was required after the event.
- *Midsight*, after some time. I became aware of the path I was headed down (Cognition) when I was in the middle of the event. I was able to intervene to get a better outcome. I was less driven and more in control.
- *Foresight*, eventually after a few months. I habitually managed my emotions and thinking prior to interactions with people, to achieve the most appropriate Behaviour. Also, I began to be more proactive about considering the psychological process and implications of matters, to prepare for a more emotionally literate outcome.

By practising, I applied the EI coaching technique to other bad habits achieving increased self-awareness at the onset. As soon as the first emotion was triggered, I thought about it and chose not to go down the habitual path of unhelpful behaviour. I felt really good about breaking these habits and it helped to reinforce new behaviour. I had built a new neural pathway and discarded the old.

Competencies for self-control

The following competencies reflect my personal view of the next step from self-awareness to self-control (although I am aware that the role of emotion in behaviour is still being examined with academic rigour).

Self-regulation: Managing emotions and holding back unhelpful impulses

To have this competency you would:
❑ stop acting on impulse when it is an unproductive behaviour
❑ remain collected, positive and unflustered even during difficult times
❑ manage distressing emotions and reduce anxiety associated with experiencing them
❑ think lucidly, remaining focused under pressure.

Authenticity: Being true to yourself and others

To have this competency you would:
❑ build trust through your reliability and congruent behaviour (words and actions are aligned)

❏ act ethically, being above reproach and questioning of your own motives
❏ admit flaws and confront unethical actions in others (zero tolerance)
❏ stand up for your values even when in the minority
❏ expect yourself to slip back occasionally and have a sense of humour and compassion about it.

Accountability: Taking responsibility, owning your performance

To have this competency you would:
❏ take responsibility for your actions and inaction where appropriate
❏ clear up miscommunication and keep promises
❏ hold yourself accountable to objectives
❏ prioritise what is important and urgent every day at work.

Flexibility: Embrace and adapt to change

To have this competency you would:
❏ take account of potential change in your planning
❏ be able to let go, accept shifting priorities and a challenging pace of change
❏ be adaptable in how you perceive events or different people
❏ be open to confronting change issues and exploring the personal implications
❏ be innovative to account for change, generating and sharing ideas.

Self-motivation: Positively managing your outlook

To have this competency you would:
- ❏ be driven to improve or meet high standards
- ❏ demonstrate commitment in all your relationships
- ❏ look for the opportunity first not the problem
- ❏ show persistence in pursuing goals and intentionality in overcoming barriers or setbacks.

Journal entries

Remember that the goal of the exercises is to learn the process of making small changes within your own limits. The purpose is not to be perfect. Be gentle with yourself if you are less than satisfied with the results.

Exercises to generate an Internal Observer
To get the benefits of EI you need to practise deconstructing the emotional roots of behaviour in routine work situations, such as team meetings.

The effectiveness and impact on stress levels is mainly due to the relationships between people in the meeting. Routine meetings are likely to have packed agendas. However, that does not mean that you cannot raise your self-awareness and other EI competencies using that as a vehicle. Prepare for your next team meeting by reflecting on past ones. Log reflections in your journal.

Looking at Low EQ in meetings

- Distraction – you are imparting information to someone but some aspect of the communication makes you aware of emotions being triggered interfering with the message. For example, you become aware that the reason you are passing this message is that you see this person fulfilling some ambition that you have personally never achieved.

- What hooks you and where you go – you are confronted by something said or being acted out by participants. You retreat into self-denial, justification, reliving past events or something else.
- Internal dialogue – you drift off listening to your inner voice because some aspect of the here and now is of insufficient interest.
- Interpretation – you make what happens in the room mean something about you whereas in reality there is no personal inference at all.
- Distraction – body language of one or more attendees shows impatience and this is transmitted to you.
- Holding back or not contributing at all.
- Outrageous attention-seeking behaviour.
- Using humour to avoid debating some real issue.

Your EQ in meetings

Look at the agenda for the meeting as far in advance as possible. Make sure that you solicit from those attending in advance any information on how the agenda items are regarded by them or by others. There is no reason why you cannot explain that you are doing some self-development around how your meetings can be more valuable. Look at the competencies described yesterday and today. Reflect on your performance at

previous meetings and decide what to work on to raise
your self-awareness and self-control.
Construct an exercise for yourself around the agenda
items in the meeting, which will allow you to practise
the competencies that you have selected. Afterwards,
record the results in your journal:
1. what happened?
2. your feelings about it?
3. what went well?
4. what you would do differently?

Tomorrow, we look at how developing your EI can be a
significant contributor to your personal stress management
strategies and practices.

Stress management and EI

Today, we are going to gain an understanding of the following topics:

- What is stress?
- Stress reactions
- Stress-related Illnesses
- Stress management strategies using EI
- Journal entries
- Stress audit

What is stress?

The word stress is derived from the Latin word 'stringere', which means to draw tight. According to Hinkle (1973), 'in the seventeenth century the word was used to describe hardship or affliction' and 'during the late eighteenth century, stress denoted force, pressure, strain or strong effort'. Cartwright & Cooper (1994) state that:

'Early definitions of strain and load used in physics and engineering eventually came to influence one concept of how stress affects individuals. Under this concept, external forces (load) are seen as exerting pressure upon an individual, producing strain.'

When survival is at risk, your body pumps in adrenaline to prepare for fight or flight. Sugars, cholesterol and fatty acids are released into the bloodstream and blood pressure and heartbeat increases. Primed for action, your body reacts with either the fight reactions of anger, aggression and hostility or the flight emotions of terror, anxiety and nervousness. The adrenaline surge is an 'upper' giving the best chance for short-term survival, a natural reaction to fear that triggers an energy level used to increase awareness and optimise performance. If you freeze when confronted with danger, that is because the necessary adrenaline is lacking.

In general, people react badly with either too little or too much stress in the long term. Without some sense of challenge (eustress or 'good' stress sensed as exhilaration and excitement) we would not get out of bed. In everyday normal stressful situations, the experience is pleasurable because one survives the threat. In basic terms, stress is an aspect of living that can be beneficial when it motivates, encourages change or inspires. It can be the opposite (distress) when it does not; individuals perceive that they do not have the resources to cope with a perceived situation from the past, present or future.

Stress reactions

The 'stress' that people complain about is a feeling of tension or pressure experienced when demands placed upon them (Stressors) are perceived as exceeding the resources they have available.

The stress cycle
The fight or flight response has been well researched and monitored. It develops in the following cycle:

- the forebrain receives danger signals from eyes, ears etc.
- the hypothalamus, in the brain, activates the pituitary gland to release hormones.

- Senses are activated, eg the pupils of the eyes dilate.
- Breathing rate increases and gets deeper. Heart rate and blood pressure increases.
- The liver releases sugar, cholesterol and fatty acids into the blood stream.
- Digestion ceases and bladder and bowel openings contract.
- The adrenal glands release hormones, adrenaline, nor-adrenaline and cortisone, which cause increased sweating and blood clotting ability.

The most common symptom is that people don't feel well and medical practitioners can find no clinical reason.

During the Stone Age, there would have been physical activity in fighting or running and the danger would have passed quickly.

In the 21st century, the body response is the same but the threats we perceive are of a financial, emotional, mental and a social nature. These types of threats are constantly present in our environment and are not generally dealt with quickly.

Stress-related illnesses

Being constantly stressed causes illness because the metabolic change is continuous, preventing relaxation or proper sleep for the body and mind to repair itself. Some long-term effects can be: hair loss, headache, migraine, strokes, impaired immune response, nervousness, bad sleeping, neck and shoulder aches, lower back and leg ache, asthma, skin conditions, high blood pressure, bad circulation, heart diseases, some cancers, indigestion, ulcers, irritable bowel syndrome, impotency, menstrual disorders and rheumatoid arthritis. The negative effects of stress can also be visible in the form of bad decision-making, negative internal politics, reduced creativity and apathy.

If optimum performance is continually maintained or surpassed (chronic stress), then performance deteriorates rapidly and people eventually become ill or die. Chronic stress is a cumulative phenomenon that can develop over a lifetime or over a few weeks. A vicious circle or rather spiral is entered into with the stress response to fear driving an individual to produce more effort for less performance, with more time spent working and less in relaxation.

Often it is not the obvious 'stress-straw' that 'breaks the camel's back'. In the working environment, chronic stress often develops from a lifestyle encouraged by employers to gain short-term competitive advantage, which then has, say, a bereavement 'straw' or house move added to it. Absenteeism generated by chronic stress can cause a 'domino' collapse of employees as each person experiences overload when coping with their own work and that of absent colleagues.

Life balance

How well do you believe you balance your time between work and play and family and employer? As often happens, if there are feelings that the balance is not right, some typical reasons may be:

- You enjoy the work.
- You fear jeopardising your career.
- You perceive that your boss expects it.
- You endure a workaholic organisational culture.
- You think that you have to prove you can cope.

Write up in your journal what you have discovered about your motivation for imbalances.

Whatever the pressures on you at work it is important to recognise the importance of relaxation and doing things that we enjoy.

Stress management strategies using EI

Like risk, stress is a perception and therefore highly personal. Here are a series of checklists of stress management measures, which, by managing what we cannot avoid and by eliminating what we can, will lead to better health.

- Manage your relationships.
- Manage your environment.
- Manage your lifestyle.
- Manage your attitude or reactions.

Manage your relationships

- Have authentic, emotionally intelligent relationships with people. Associate with those whose company you enjoy and who support you. Authenticity requires self-awareness and emotional expression so that when in conversation with an individual you are able to share your feelings openly, including any distractions impairing your ability to concentrate on them. The relationship would be equitable and based on a sense of mutuality. While the degree of give and take may vary from time to time based on your needs, it would find an agreed equilibrium. When worries start to build up, talk to someone with whom you have a close relationship.
- Learn how to have assertive conversations with those who create anxiety by not acknowledging your feelings and rights. As much as possible, clear your life of people who drain your emotional battery creating unacceptable anxiety and conflict. Don't drift along in troublesome and distressing situations or relationships. Take action to change rather than trying to avoid the problem or deny it exists. Taking chances is the key to emotional well-being.
- Protect your personal freedoms and space. Do what you want and feel, but respect the rights of others. Don't tell others what to do, but if they intrude, let them know.
- Set up a co-coaching relationship with someone you trust, preferably someone with coaching experience. Meet at least once a month, split the time and have a scheduled

phone call every week. Select life-improving books to read and share together. Tackle real issues including denial and avoidance with each other. Use your journal entries and prepare for the co-coaching sessions, writing the results up at the time and after reflection. Note the advice on coaching in Friday's chapter.

- Watch your conversations for faulty thought patterns, such as selective envy, disaster forecasting, finding the scapegoat, generalisation and projecting our reactions onto others.

Manage your environment

For one week, log in your journal notes about changes to your stress levels and the environment you are in at the time.

- Being ruthless, identify the Stressors and think what you can do about them (for example, clutter in the house, shed and garage, or your journeys to work, or the lack of a study or 'den' for you).

- Surround yourself with cues from positive thoughts and relaxation.
- Find a time and place each day where you can have complete privacy. Take time off from others and pressures.

Manage your lifestyle
Change your lifestyle by removing the causes of stress. Look at the following.

- Effective time management is just one of many ways to keep from succumbing to stress overload. Make time to learn and practice relaxation or meditation skills.
- Engage in a vigorous physical exercise that is convenient and pleasurable. Check with your doctor before engaging on a new programme if you are unused to it. Sometimes it helps to get a friend to exercise with you to keep the discipline.
- Short breaks during the day (every 45 minutes if working at a computer) can help improve efficiency and well-being the rest of the day. In addition, the breaks help with avoidance of problems with posture (lower back syndrome), eyesight and Repetitive Strain Injuries (RSI).
- Maintain a reasonable diet and sane sleeping habits. Use alcohol and medication wisely; you must be in control of them not vice versa. Avoid the use of sleeping pills, tranquillisers and other drugs to control stress (exercise really helps with sleeping problems as does a diet that acknowledges foods that can stimulate you throughout the day or encourage sleep at night.)

Manage your attitude
We are not upset by things but rather the view we take of
them.   Epictetus

You may have a positive attitude to something that is causing you and others around you stress. It may be a weakness because of its extreme nature when it could be moderated and become a strength. Apart from the need to balance life and career, our personal characteristics play an important role in creating stress. Seek the view of others on the characteristics that might add to your stress, such as:

- perfectionism
- misdirected anxiety
- need for approval of others
- pessimism
- impatience
- a wish to avoid conflict
- poor opinion of self.

If we wish to avoid undue stress we must recognise the role such characteristics play and be prepared to modify our values. Reflect on this and write the results up in your journal.

Because of the way an EI programme is structured (covered on Thursday and Friday), it allows people to build the skills to reduce stress on a continual basis. Returning to the programme outcomes every three months over a one-year period enables progress to be reviewed. Developmental areas can be shared and from this, creative solutions generated. Working with a group rewards the new behaviours being instilled. Shortly, we will look at a stress audit that can start you on this programme as a diagnostic phase.

An EI approach to reducing stress
You might want to experiment to see what works best for you. An emotionally intelligent approach to tackling stress includes:

- Increasing competencies in self-awareness, self-control and in awareness of others.
- Viewing life as challenges to seek and not as obstacles to avoid. Review your obligations from time to time and make sure they are still good for you, if they're not, let them go.
- Using assertiveness through a balance of responsive and assertive behaviours.
- Identifying positive approaches to events, rather than just worrying with negative thoughts.
- Understanding the true cost of our values and beliefs.
- Not becoming one-dimensional; don't let one thing dominate you, such as a current project, schoolwork, relationships, career, sports, hobby etc.
- Opening yourself to fresh experiences; try new-fangled things, novel foods and new places; take responsibility for your life and your feelings, but never blame yourself. Ownership of your life is a better philosophy than a blame culture.

Journal entries

Stress audit

Write down the answers to the following questions in your journal:

- Do you ever feel unable to cope?
- Do you find it difficult to relax?
- Do you ever feel anxious for no reason?
- Do you find it hard to show your true feelings?
- Are you finding it hard to make decisions?
- Are you often irritable for no reason?
- Do you worry about the future?
- Do you feel isolated and misunderstood?
- Do you doubt that you like yourself?
- Are you finding it difficult to concentrate?
- Do you find that life has lost its sparkle?
- I believe that for me stress is . . .
- Some Stressors in my life are:
  - ❑ Life pressures
  - ❑ Life satisfactions
  - ❑ General health
  - ❑ Quality of life
  - ❑ Relationships
- What do you see as you at your best (for example, if you are perfectionist you may be driving yourself too hard because you believe that you are at your best when actually striving for the impossible)?
- In the past 12 months the most challenging or exciting event in my life was . . .
- In the past 12 months the following event(s) was/were quite stressful . . .

Using the definitions of self-awareness and self-control in the last two chapters, together with the insight discovered in looking at the stress audit, explore how EQ competencies can help you. This allows you to assess the impact of raising EQ on stress-reduction not only within your organisation and working team but also in your home life.

Remember that the goal of the exercises is to learn the process of making small changes within your own limits. The purpose is not to be perfect. Be gentle with yourself when you are less than satisfied with the results. Record the results in your journal and review.

What will my company gain from an investment in EI?

Today, we are going to gain an understanding of the following topics:

Investment in EI
How to create an EI culture:

- – EI culture change project life cycle
- – Stage 1: Creating the EI team
- – Stage 2: Diagnosing and exploring change in your organisation
- – Stage 3: Closure of issues
Journal entries
- – Actions to ensure success

Investment in EI

Many people have a passion to reinvent their organisation. I suggest here that creating an EI culture can be part of that reinvention. If you want to change the world, start by changing yourself. 'You have to **be** the change you wish for the world' (Gandhi). Firstly, let's understand the business context by looking at a common scenario. In the 20th century, HR specialists sought to generate a 'Performance Culture' in their organisation by applying personal and management development methods:

- to produce measures that help the frontline to do anything faster, better, cheaper; or
- to produce measures that are clear enablers, neither barriers nor things that hamper operations.

This would work well with other initiatives, such as:

- Total Quality Management, a model of world-class excellence
- Customer Relationship Management (CRM) models and Relationship Marketing
- Six Sigma philosophy (very few errors) and Agile manufacturing (flexible production)
- other benchmarking or transformational initiatives.

You also have to generate differentiating products and services. However, I believe an EI culture can remove the friction that holds you back and can provide emotional stamina to tackle global challenges.

People in business will have to achieve standards of excellence that routinely compete in a global market. Twenty-first century companies are moving away from 'Product Push' to 'Relationship Pull'. HR people will be faced with leaders who hire people solely for knowledge and task-orientation not their way of 'being' with customers, suppliers and colleagues. Does this sound familiar to you?

I believe that EI will define success in the 21st century, *doing* more will not be enough – *being* different might achieve the highest goals.

We lose customers as well as staff for EQ-related reasons. In other words, we deliver superior products but the service aspect is lacking in some way.

It is 16 times cheaper to sell another product or service to an existing customer than to find a new client. It makes hard cash sense to expend effort in not only retaining existing satisfied customers but in converting them to advocates. Creating advocacy brings an average of five new customers at very low cost of acquisition. A dissatisfied customer will tell three times more people about you than an advocate. 15 people will be put off using your product or service – that is very expensive.

How is this related to improvements in EQ? If the cause of complaint is explored and the customer handled using great self-control, awareness and influencing skills a transformation can be achieved – even a conversion to an advocate. Successful customer-facing staff display a high degree of emotional literacy (Tuesday) in creating sustainable, profitable relationships with customers. The collection of high-quality and comprehensive information for marketing and R&D purposes requires excellent social skills and awareness of others.

> **The cost of low EQ**
>
> Think back to Sunday and the three incidents involving
> a customer/supplier relationship.
> - Think back to the exchanges between people.
> - Have a go at looking at the costs involved in the
>   outcome.
> - Can you see that higher EQ here can lead to
>   sustainable, profitable relationships with customers
>   and cheaper customer acquisition?
> - What would this look like for your company?

*Positive affirmation – a milestone in an Emotionally Intelligent
culture*

One of the ways to **be** different is to bring up a child to be an
emotionally intelligent adult using positive affirmation.
Without this, the emergent adult will be without the skills at
work to generate and participate in a beneficial climate. This
is more sophisticated than saying please and thank you for
tasks performed well. Over two decades, Daniel Goleman
(original book, *Emotional Intelligence*, 1995) studied a decline
in the EQ of young people, sadly evidenced by violence in
schools stemming from unresolved relationships and unmet
emotional needs.

The reasons why the practice of positive affirmation is a
milestone in an emotionally intelligent culture are:

- It brings rewards, such as netting undiscovered potential,
  into the workplace.
- It allows teams to celebrate more and be positive with a
  regular sense of well-being.

- It avoids the language of human deficit that blocks cultures like cholesterol clogs arteries.
- It has beneficial effects, such as opening up brain function.
- Combined with heightened emotional states and other techniques designed to take advantage of brain function, positive affirmation can be embedded in one instance of learning (it does not have to be repeated many times to stick).

Consider the above bullets and come up with ideas on how to achieve them. Record in your journal your reaction to your answers and any thoughts regarding them.

People are not naturally prone to giving positive feedback (Wheldall and Merrett). This varies from culture to culture and it may strike more of a note with different individuals. Adults need to be educated to unlearn years of being covertly rewarded for cutting people down to size. Working in a culture that does not positively re-enforce, feedback becomes associated solely with negative comments. In this climate, praise is given in a vacuum of detail. Criticism is remembered with 20/20 vision *forever*.

For praise to achieve its aim there is a requirement to give specific evaluative feedback. This lets people know what they have done; in particular, so that good behaviours become ingrained. However, it is not unusual for managers to overplay the 'exceeds expectations' grading in performance appraisals due to fear of accurate feedback being construed as unsupported criticism. On the occasions that positive feedback is given, it is not given rigorously and systematically, ie in a way that is going to change people's behaviour. To change the adult, you may have to revisit the child within, such as:

- the climate in which they were brought up,
- which behaviours were rewarded and how overtly or covertly,
- which behaviours were punished.

There is an approach to positive feedback (producing a positive culture, up-skilling employees and improving retention) that would allow an EI culture to be created. Designed to empower people to facilitate behaviour change, I recommend that this becomes part of the induction programme and that existing managers are coached in the skills. In order to ensure a powerful impact on the organisation, both a training course and ongoing coaching would be required.

How to create an EI culture

In this and the next chapter, we are going to look at how to create an EI culture.

EI culture change project life cycle
A typical life cycle for an EI culture change project has the following stages (run in parallel to some degree using different resources):

Stage 1: Creating the EI team
Stage 2: Diagnosing and exploring change in your organisation
Stage 3: Closure of issues surrounding the old culture and discovering the new culture
Stage 4: Two-way communication of the dream or vision for the new EI culture
Stage 5: Designing a programme to deliver the dream or

vision, including what has to be given up

Stage 6: Piloting the design pragmatically

Stage 7: Reviewing the pilot and matching the results against expectations

Stage 8: Completing the cycle for the rest of the organisation

Stage 1: Creating the EI team

With businesses under pressure financially and competitively, it is not a good idea to utilise consultants on repeated activities that could be done by internal or specialist staff after they have been given extra capabilities. To be economic, a 'Forest Fire' approach is expedient (starts from a point selected by external experts and is spread outwards by a handpicked internal EI team).

The EI team is composed of those with good facilitation skills and an affiliative approach, selected from:

- the Organisational Development team
- HR or Training and Development teams
- volunteers – inspired individuals dedicated to reinventing the organisation (but check how you are going to select them for suitability)
- external consultants hired for expertise to transfer knowledge and skills by training and coaching the internal EI team.

The EI team members may need to go through a formal assessment process to get the mix right for the programme. The skills of these individuals could be raised by a number of interventions: coaching and assessment, paired facilitation of others, regular feedback and Continuous Professional Development (CPD).

If available funding is extremely low, a bespoke Train The EI Coach course can be developed and delivered by the HR Manager (or project sponsor if that role is going to be very hands-on). This course should include how to evaluate the potential of the EI team back in their new role.

Developed to become resilient EI change agents and coaches, members must be able to cope well with participants enduring the agonies of raising themselves through the learning ladder (see Sunday). During workshop sessions, specific change issues will impact participant's lives. They will be confronted by what it means for them to meet the new demands of the business.

Rolling it out as a pilot programme, the EI team would transfer change agency to managers and staff as quickly as possible with expert guidance as required.

After creating the EI team, I recommend that you begin with a diagnostic phase in order to understand the current organisational culture. This provides an opportunity to finalise the way forward.

Stage 2: Diagnosing and exploring change in your organisation
Run through the checklist below thinking about your current organisation. Which of them can you tick without any doubts in your mind?

Organisational checklist

☐ My organisation has a strategic view.

☐ Senior people energise others lower in the system.

☐ Leaders here create a structure that follows function.

☐ Managers make decisions at a point when the relevant information is held or comes together.

☐ This company has a reward system that balances what you know and what you do.

☐ We have relatively open communication.

☐ We reward collaboration when it is in the organisation's best interests.

☐ Our managers manage conflict, they do not suppress it.

☐ Our leaders view the organisation as an open system and manage the demands put upon it.

☐ Our organisation values individuality and individuals.

☐ We actively learn through feedback.

The above checklist is part of a Healthy Organisation Checklist by Beckhard in his work *Organisational Transitions – Managing Complex Change*. The more ticks indicates the greater health of your organisation. Record in your journal your reaction to each answer and any thoughts regarding reinvention. You could consider the above checklist to be a series of milestones for entry into a change management plan for the EI culture change project.

If you have ticked all of them then you are fortunate to work in an organisation that is emotionally literate and shares learning. I recommend that you share the checklist with as many people as possible to come up with a joint diagnosis. You will be unable to mobilise people to change without such agreement.

Diagnosing change

- Thinking about change in your organisation, what kind of change do you want in the following areas?

  > Organisational policies
  > Leadership styles
  > Environment
  > Relationships
  > Processes, procedures or practices
  > Attitudes
  > Behaviour

- For each of the above, who needs to be involved?
- How ready or fit for change is your organisation?
- How prepared is it for the changes you want?
- Who or what are the forces for and against the changes?
- How realistic are the changes you want?
- How can you modify your change needs to make them more realistic?
- What resources can you tap into?

  > Help from Government, such as grants, cheap loans, agencies and business schemes
  > Central resources as part of a group or larger organisation

---

Internal teams set up for this purpose
Volunteers? How will you measure their
suitability?

- Thinking of your organisation at present:

  Which part is most vulnerable to change from
  external drivers?
  Which part is most vulnerable to change from
  internal drivers?

Record the answers in your journal. If you do not know the
answers then enquire into how a change process might be
initiated in your organisation. People often feel safer doing
some exploration about what change would feel like and
how it could happen. See Stage 3 as mandatory if you are in
this situation.

*Stage 3: Closure of issues surrounding the old culture and
discovering the new culture*
For the want of a stage like this, many culture change
programmes fail to achieve a critical mass of transformation.
Most leaders and HR partners initiate programmes in the
shadow of programmes gone before. Common business
scenarios for this are new ventures, mergers and acquisitions.

In order for a company's staff to alter both attitudes and
behaviour, they need to understand the purpose and benefits
of the change ('What's in it for me'). Research into
organisational change shows that without this understanding
people may *appear* to change without fundamentally altering
their attitudes or behaviour. It is safer for them to stay where
they are in terms of mindset. Without full buy-in from
necessary staff, people may even sabotage the new culture.

In order to support this whole process of generating an EI culture, it is vital for staff to let go of allegiance to the previous culture. There may be a good deal to be given up in the way of unproductive behaviours to which work-based teams are attached (albeit unknowingly). There is always a payoff for behaving in these ways, such as:

- Getting to be right.
- Playing the cynic and never having to commit to anything.
- Dominating or bullying others.
- Self-justification.
- Blaming others and not being responsible.
- Martyrdom – professional victims frequently switch places and persecute their victimiser.

When a new approach is adopted people may feel that previous work goes unrecognised, which may stop them supporting the new ideas and methods. They may not even be aware of previous beliefs and actions; it is possible for cultures to be implicit rather than explicit. What is needed is to be clear about the present culture, lay it to rest and model the new. Without this fundamental step, change will not occur.

You need to discover what values people are wedded to on a daily basis and how they compare with any new values. If they sense you view the old culture as wrong and the reason for moving forward is to put things right, this does not give credit for what has worked. Many people may have taken to heart a previous mission, vision and values. Start with praise for what has been achieved to date to show respect and to translate the success to the new paradigm collaboratively through skilled facilitation. This ensures that there is no talk of the past being wrong or the results unwanted. In addition, it is vital that the reward and remuneration mechanisms are updated to incentivise the new behaviours.

Regenerate enthusiasm for the organisation moving to the next stage of advancement by checking the sense of 'permission to proceed'. The status of permission may be manifest in hard management decisions on financial approvals for consultancy or for staff being released from operations for change events. It is essentially a contracting issue for the EI team whose mission it is to change the organisation with those who officially (and unofficially) hold sway in the organisation. We'll continue these stages tomorrow.

Journal entries

Study the following actions to ensure success and make notes in your journal on how they apply to your organisation.

Actions to ensure success
1 Make sure that all relevant employees are clear about the previous culture.
2 Celebrate the past achievements by providing opportunities for them to feel acknowledged for what they've done well.
3 Avoid any elitism of the Executive having higher paid coaches than the workforce.

How to create an EI culture

Today, we are going to continue (from yesterday) exploring
how to create an EI culture as follows:

How to create an EI culture

- Stage 4:   Two-way communication of the dream
- Stage 5:   Designing a programme to deliver the
              dream
- Stage 6:   Piloting the design pragmatically
- Stage 7:   Reviewing the pilot
- Stage 8:   Completing the cycle

Journal entries
-         Learning organisation mind map
-         Example programme outcomes

Stage 4: Two-way communication of the dream or vision for the new EI culture

The communication must be effective both ways reporting
from top to bottom and vice versa:

- The strategy must enrol all staff in the new approach
  clearly stating the benefits, including financial ones, and
  speculative risks.
- The strategy must ensure that there is sponsorship of the
  new culture by those with power in the organisation.

Actively increase 'shop floor' participation using skills
transferred from change agents. Plan to reduce over time the

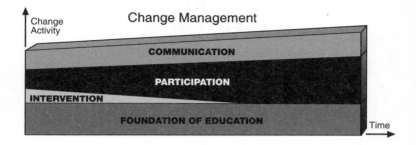

scale of intervention by change agents, managers, consultants or trainers. Do not reduce the effort for Continuous Professional Development, education or communication.

It is often economic to bring in experienced executives who can model the new behaviours and it is not unusual for senior executives who cannot to elect to leave.

Stage 5: Designing a programme to deliver the dream

A culture change project designed to be sustainable and profitable for the company should start with a self-awareness programme (Step 1 overleaf). If staff are not able to see themselves as others see them, it is pointless attempting to raise their social skills and awareness of others.

The five-step EI team programme
I recommend a five-step training and development process laid out below. I would suggest that a pivotal goal is that the EI team creates a 'critical mass' of advocates and exemplars of the new culture. It is essential that this programme be considered a business priority. The whole company should

be put through as many of the steps as can be afforded with a recommended minimum of the two marked with an asterisk.

Step 1 ***Foundation** – Self-awareness and knowledge about own EI competencies (see Monday). Identification of a first set of unproductive behaviours and commitment to change through development back in the workplace.

Step 2 ***Generating an Internal Observer** – Using increased self-awareness from Step 1 to increase self-control by identifying the emotional triggers to unproductive behaviour: enhancing self-regulation, authenticity, accountability, flexibility and self-motivation (see Tuesday).

Step 3 **Change agency and stress management (see Wednesday)** – Using Steps 1 and 2 to understand sources of stress, to generate and commit to stress management strategies. To understand and utilise change management techniques suitable for self, use with others and organisationally.

Step 4 **Conflict management, negotiation and assertive behaviour** – Influencing strategies and techniques are explored to resolve conflict equitably, to reconcile differences in negotiations and to practise assertive behaviour.

Step 5 **Developing specific EI coaching skills using a seven-step coaching process and method** (see *Effective Coaching* by Marshall J Cook).

　　5.1　**Contracting phase** – The challenge faced by the

coachee and the required outcome are identified. The contract for the coaching relationship is explored and the commitment is made.

5.2 **The coaching approach** - Possible approaches to the coaching process are brainstormed based on understanding of the context of the challenge as well as the employees' personal issues. Lateral thinking is encouraged and unconventional ideas given consideration.

5.3 **The action plan** - The first meeting needs to complete some time management and the practical aspects of the coaching environment. What type of environment is suitable to the nature of the challenge (complete privacy needed or relative privacy of noisy public venue)? What aids might be needed if any?

5.4 **Agree deadlines** - What is the schedule and arrangements for changing it (revisit contract if required)?

5.5 **Evaluation** - What are the criteria for evaluation of success? How will the coachee know when the coaching is working? When will the coach establish that his or her subject is not coachable on this topic?

5.6 **Facilitate action** – What can you as coach do to help your employees succeed? Facilitation involves avoiding being tempted to rescue employees, thus stealing their autonomy of action and thought. Paternalistic or maternalistic approaches that take over the task from the employee are diametrically opposed to the coaching approach.

5.7 **Follow through** – This is a collaborative way of enforcing deadlines and setting time to review progress to ensure well-intentioned plans do not get lost.

Working with the executive layer, the programme may be re-iterated with the first batch becoming 'super coaches'. Coherent management of the change programme can be achieved by merging EI competencies with hard managerial and analytical skills. (There is room for the emotionally intelligent Project Manager to report progress culturally).

EI learning methodology

The programme should focus on generating opportunities for experiential learning, sharing knowledge of EI and change agency. Examples of the diverse learning methodologies are deployed in both classroom – and work-based environments, as set out below.

Classroom-based work
By being very interactive, participants practise the skills they are developing through a variety of training methods, which meet delegates' varying learning styles. These include:

- a variety of accelerated learning techniques, presentations, debates and exercises to help practise new skills and knowledge
- activities allowing delegates to develop understanding of themselves and the ways they interact with others, eg role-plays and games to understand how they relate to colleagues and customers (both internal and external), or team building exercises to facilitate support of each other in their new role.

Development at work
Working with the business to embed EI coaching in the culture and processes, developmental learning back at work should be provided to ensure success within the work context. Exercises should be designed to fit in with routine events in the workplace, for example team meetings described in Monday and Tuesday. This will include the following:

- learning sets, crossfunctional teams, focus groups or workshops, eg ways of developing structures to generate the EI programme internally

- directed self-study, one-to-one or team coaching sessions for shared EI exercises
- facilitated e-rooms to share knowledge and experience (if you have the technology and are globally disparate).

Learning outcomes for EI culture change interventions
People behave as they are rewarded. Organisations waste money by charging ahead with training while delaying renegotiations of company pay, rewards and remuneration. Alignment of reward mechanisms to the learning outcomes is essential in Stage 5. Mismatches are very disillusioning for participants.

In order for participants to continue to adopt a positive approach throughout the organisation, it is important that they have coaching immediately following each course. It would be helpful if their consolidation successes are recognised (rewards, reviews, appraisal etc).

Learning outcomes of the five-step programme

By the end of the programme, the EI team will have achieved all the learning outcomes. They will:

- Have a growing capability in self-awareness and self-control, successfully managing themselves in challenging situations, creating more effective teams and positively impacting on organisational culture and morale.
- Develop further their interpersonal skills, eg assertiveness, influencing skills, rapport building etc.
- Recognise how they develop 'unhelpful' baggage about some of their colleagues and be able to self-assess their present approach to feedback to employees and have discussed the present organisational culture; understanding how to use positive feedback in order to change behaviour and improving their strategies to consistently generate positive feedback.
- Understand the purpose of EI coaching and analyse their strengths and areas of development as coaches and respect the autonomy of coachees in action and thought; being able to use their skills to know when coaching or other more directive-styles of leadership approaches is required.

Stage 6: Piloting the design pragmatically

Do not select the worst region because you want to change it the most and think that this will form a useful pilot. Your consultant team may well be experienced enough to tackle this region but your new EI coaches may find it too big a step. This will be demoralising and you need to start with a winner. In surrounding regions that have taken the transformation well and have emotional stamina, you can always restructure (each absorbing parts of the difficult region) using the critical mass.

Make sure that you have consulted all stakeholders on the pilot evaluation criteria. Be clear that you know what good looks like in the new behavioural competencies in the opinion of all the key decision-makers. To sustain the new culture it is essential that those who will judge competence are reliable and consistent.

Usually consultants 'start the fire' and teach others how to spread it with a wedge of resources that reduces with time. The goal is for the EI team to transfer all of their knowledge and skills to the business as well as creating opportunities for experiential learning. The approach will only be successful if the recipients pick up all of the skills needed from the consultants and do not dilute the messages.

It is wise for the EI team to remain ahead of the learning curve to maintain a gap between them and the main body of personnel. They are then able to support staff stopping any cultural shear between personnel, supervisors, middle managers and the executive level.

During the transition phase, EI team members would be coached to ensure that they have understood the models, practice and experience of EI coaching. The transition phase would be to complete the transfer of knowledge. Evaluation would be a continuous process; thereby ensuring business needs are met.

The pilot would then be used to decide to what scale external support remains necessary and to complete the implementation plan for the wider organisation based on success.

Stage 7: Reviewing the pilot

I would not expect to see financial pay back in less than 12 months. However, within three months I would expect individuals to evidence and report personal perceptions of benefit. They may be able to quote specific examples where use of their new EI competencies generated new business, protected existing business or increased sales, eg handling customer complaints. A potentially dissatisfied customer can be converted to an advocate if the complaint is handled really well.

The programme would include a diagnostic stage for both the individuals and the organisation. Classroom-based work and other developmental approaches would follow this. Trainee coaches would be given individual coaching throughout to ensure that they have understood the models, practice and experience of coaching.

Stage 8: Completing the cycle

There are too many variables to give detailed advice here other than some general guidelines.

- Right from the start, have a communications strategy that uses formal and informal chains of communication.
- Plan the change programme professionally paying equal

attention to the psychological process that people will go through, as you do to the tasks, goals and techniques employed.

- Ideally, everyone in the company should receive at least the first two courses concentrating on achieving heightened self-awareness and a capability to use this awareness to increase self-control. Each of these should then be followed by a period of development back in the workplace.

- Put first-line supervisors through the programme first if you have to limit the volume. You can afford to leave middle management until quite late but not executives, specialists or first-line supervisors as they generate more risk if they are living the old culture.

- Have a feedback loop that evaluates comments from participants carefully, remembering where they are on the learning ladder. Participants can kick out at trainers and change agents when the subject matter is confronting because it is below their level of self-awareness (they do not know what they do not know). Anticipate this and have change techniques to hand, being prepared to give individuals extra coaching (refer back to the five-step course for EI Team).

- Do not be surprised if strong bonds emerge between the EI coaches and participants on their courses. Collaborative approaches between first line supervisors and the EI team will make the transition back to work seamless. Make the transition work by a process of encouraging supervisors to coach people emerging from courses, and by the EI team coaching the supervisors.

- Complete risk management exercises at three levels: business (speculative or good risks where you are speculating to accumulate), programme level (where many projects interact and are dependent) and the individual project level where they vary depending on the nature (Information System, building move, training life-cycle).

Key influencers and leaders in the business must reinforce the new culture. Methods of continuing the development of the organisation include:

- learning sets to tackle remaining cultural issues and to develop processes
- crossfunctional teams to ensure that processes do not stumble at the internal interfaces and that the new behaviours do not get reinterpreted within boundaries
- self-directed teams within workgroups to conduct continuous improvement without over-heavy management intervention
- benchmarking clubs to think laterally across market sectors to generate ideas and best practice
- strategic approaches to business such as customer relationship management where the boundaries of the organisation are breached and you are truly in the shoes of your customer.

Journal entries

Learning organisation mind map
Consider the following diagram in relation to your own organisation and what you would like to achieve with it. I believe that the EI programme can go a long way towards achieving the advantages of being a learning organisation. In your journal, taking a clockwise scan around the mind map, reflect on:

- where your organisation is at present
- where it wants to be and by when
- how it might get there.

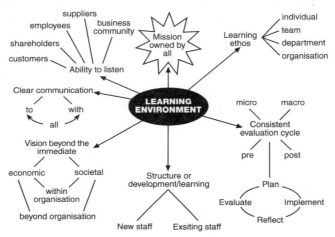

Developed by Cathie Woodward BA (Hons) BPhil MA

Use the information to reflect on the programme outline in Thursday and today to develop a plan bespoke to your organisation's needs.

Develop a range of programme outcomes that you would like to achieve.

Example programme outcomes

The ability to:
- identify and develop better leaders, maximising productivity and reducing turnover of staff
- gain advantage from systemic learning, continuous improvement, learning sets, crossfunctional and self-directed teams

Today, we have covered the final part of how to create an EI culture. You should have enough information to work with internal teams and consultants on your own programme. Tomorrow, we are going to review the week developing a Personal Development Plan based on what we have learned.

Preparing for the next developmental steps

Today, we are going to explore what you might do after completing this book, by gaining an understanding of the following topics:

- The value of keeping a journal
- What a Personal Development Plan is and why it is useful
- Guidelines for completing a professional development analysis
- Designing a programme for you
- Steps in development

The value of keeping a journal

On Sunday, we covered the format for a journal entry and some experience concerning the value of doing so. The idea of keeping a journal is to consistently log your learning, keeping the information in one place readily to hand, and thus making it as easy as possible to do this. Alternatively, use the following formats and keep the logs in your Personal Development Plan folder:

- Learning log questionnaire
- Emotional Intelligence Exercise log.

Give details of your role at that time and whether you are being supervised in thie activities. Then record answers to the following bullets:

Log

- Learning goals being worked on.

- Record of the last exercise completed.

- What learning occurred?

- List your main strengths and weaknesses during the exercise.

- What learning goals do you wish to continue working on?

Emotional Intelligence exercise log
Create a simple four-column table, Exercise number, Date completed, With whom and Remarks. Leave whole rows between the exercises, so you can repeat each exercise with different people.

What a Personal Development Plan is and why it is useful

A PDP should start with a baseline entry that may be developed using some techniques, such as a professional development analysis. Guidelines are given for this below. The PDP should be maintained throughout training. If possible, it can be updated every day using the learning outcomes, session objectives or teaching points as a structure. The status of personal development should be judged against agreed criteria for every job.

Any gaps identified can be developed through a variety of methods, such as coaching and formal learning events. The choices available have been described earlier in the week.

If your organisation conducts 360° appraisals feeding into your PDP, try to keep the identification of gaps in a positive framework. If it becomes known that this process is always used to elicit weaknesses that are used in performance-related pay, then the shared insights will become defensive in nature. This will prevent a healthy learning pattern forming.

Guidelines for completing a professional development analysis

SWOT
Complete a SWOT table of four quadrants which considers:

- Internal factors – Consider the strengths and weaknesses in specialist, technical and business skills plus personal effectiveness.
- External Opportunities & Threats – Consider the impact of environmental drivers & personal factors including lifestyle plans.

You might like to consider those areas of weakness important to the business or to you personally. Similarly in respect of your strengths, there may be a business opportunity that requires you to develop one or more of these further, ie to expert level. Strengths and weaknesses must be considered in the light of the opportunities and threats.

Competency analysis
This involves identifying those capabilities required for a job or future aspiration. Identify the skills, knowledge and experience that are required to successfully meet the current and future requirements of your role and record them in a table such as the one opposite.

Competency analysis table				
Skills, knowledge and experience required for job or future aspirations	Important/ urgent	Current level 1–5	Target level	Gap

Skills are usually acquired through training interventions away from work and on-the-job training. You can ask to be given projects to tackle real organisational issues and to acquire experience not prevalent in your current role, in order to broaden your development. You can acquire knowledge through training and a number of development options, including self-study, learning sets, crossfunctinal teams, and through use of learning technologies.

Important/urgent grading
Score each skill according to its importance and urgency. Recognise what motivates you and expect it to have a higher priority. However, you may decide that a skill is less important but as part of personal growth you still wish to give it a high priority.

In addition to the above imperatives, identify those skills you might like to develop that will enrich or broaden you professionally and personally.

Competency – current level and target level
Grade your current level of competencey on a scale of 1-5 and then define the target level that you would like to achieve.

5 (Expert) – Practising at a level of excellence with high

degree of skill and vast knowledge base

4 (Practitioner) – Proficient and above minimum standard required due to experience and advanced knowledge

3 (Foundation) – Meets minimum standard of competence, familiar and able to use relevant knowledge and skill

2 (Basic) – Some or little knowledge/skill, but unable to practise at a competent level

1 (Novice) – No knowledge/skill, requires extensive training.

Gap

Having identified your current and target level of competence, determine the gap (difference) between the two levels. This figure will help you form a basis to identify those skills that require professional development.

Summary

Having completed the SWOT and competency analysis consider those aspects requiring development, taking into consideration:

- the scale of gap based on the analysis of your skills, experience and knowledge
- how important, urgent or critical they are to your current role or future aspirations.

Break down any large gaps into stages to make them manageable. Be realistic and identify what is achievable to be motivating.

Consider further self-appraisal and feedback from clients, colleagues, mentors and others on your behaviour and emotional knowledge.

Designing a programme for you

To design a programme for you, you need to understand your learning preferences and prejudices.

From Monday you will appreciate that raising EQ is possible because EI is learnable. If you are really in tune with your needs, then you will find it easier to tackle the kind of learning involved in raising your EQ. We indicated that there are two types of learning: cognitive and emotional. Revisit the chapter if you have lost the distinction.

The prospect of needing to develop greater EI is likely to generate resistance to change.

If you have not done so already, you can do an assessment of your preferred learning style using the work of Kolb (*Learning Styles*), which indicates your range of styles; Activist, Reflector, Theorist or Pragmatist.

Emotional Intelligence 'tests' have been developed by a number of researchers but there is no single view of what EI is; there are a number of different views. Although the reader should not allow their focus to remain on measurement, it is useful to measure EQ with an assessment at the start of EI development and about one year into it.

Here is a list of some of the better-known gurus covered in Test Your Emotional Intelligence. There are many arguments for each different nuance but the core argument is the same: you can develop yourself to have better self-regulation and to use your senses to enhance your success in relationships with others. A number of 'tests' are available on the Internet if you use the search engines. However, the following are more robust scientifically-based instruments from individual researchers, backed by organisations developing and supplying the instruments. Assessments are available from:

1 Reuven Bar-On
2 Richard Cooper and Ayman Sawaf
3 Dulewicz and Higgs
4 Daniel Goleman
5 Mayer, Salovey and Caruso.

Steps in development

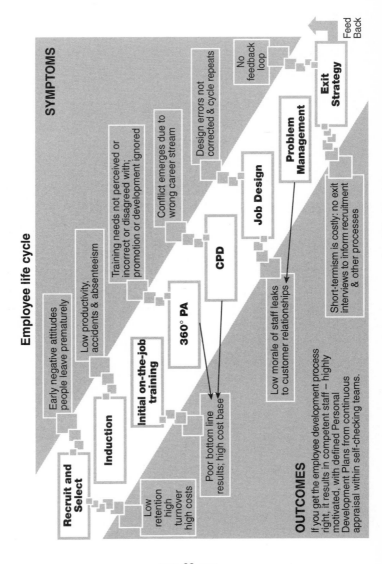

Employee life cycle

SYMPTOMS

Feed Back

No feedback loop

Exit Strategy

Design errors not corrected & cycle repeats

Problem Management

Conflict emerges due to wrong career stream

Job Design

Training needs not perceived or incorrect or disagreed with; promotion or development ignored

CPD

Early negative attitudes people leave prematurely

Low productivity, accidents & absenteeism

360° PA

Initial on-the-job training

Induction

Recruit and Select

Low morale of staff leaks to customer relationships

Short-termism is costly: no exit interviews to inform recruitment & other processes

Poor bottom line results; high cost base

Low retention high turnover high costs

OUTCOMES

If you get the employee development process right, it results in competent staff – highly motivated, with defined Personal Development Plans from continuous appraisal within self-checking teams.

Following the employee life cycle, your PDP should be started on joining your first organisation. It needs to be updated at every step and used as a guide for the rest of your career. For example:

1. Induction and initial business training.
2. On-the-job rehearsal (sitting-next-to-Nelly).
3. Coaching.
4. Continuous learning through Continuous Professional Development, including structures for developing further line responsibility by embedding reward and remuneration into the process.
5. Validation of materials and accreditation of individual's learning by an appropriate academic institution.
6. Two-way communication between your own company and other global brand leaders to maximise learning.

Creating a structure – prepare, conduct, reflect

Experience of running EI programmes has led me to the conclusion that inviting people to carry out further tasks after training dooms development. Even the most careful contracting in the world is challenged by the impact of the climate when people return to work from learning events. I suggest a more lateral approach:

- improve the work environment to make learning a part of your business as usual
- make doing development activities a way of preparing, conducting and reflecting on routine events at work.

Rather than add items to your in tray, use the EI development exercises contained in this book to prepare, conduct and reflect on everyday events. The concept is that the way you are 'being' about your life will be different, rather than the way you deploy an additional or alternative technique or your task-orientation.

Plan to run exercises in as many relationships as possible seeking collaboration with others and using the book to set the context if others are anxious.

Conclusion

Emotions are not merely the remnant of our pre-sapient past but rather they form important characteristics of an active, searching and thinking human being. Anything that is a novelty, a discrepancy or an interruption generates a visceral response, while our cognitive system interprets the world as threatening, exciting, frightening or joyful.

The human world is so replete with emotions, not because we are animals at heart, but because it is so full of things that elate or threaten us. With new research into the nature of emotional experience and expression, it is possible to enquire into the role of emotions in adaptive behaviour.

- If Darwin was right, what will be the process of Natural Selection for humans in the 21st century and will Emotional Intelligence have been a positive selection factor?
- Of those organisations that adapt to survive, which will endure and why?

I hope that you will conclude (as I did) that, once started, developing your EQ becomes a lifelong enquiry into the joys and mysteries of being human.